New Zealand Edible Garden

Published 2000 by Hyndman Publishing
325 Purchas Road
RD 2
Amberly 7482
ISBN 1-877168-46-7

TEXT:	© Bill Ward
CONCEPT & FORMAT:	Neil Hyndman
LAYOUT & DESIGN:	Dileva Design Ltd
PHOTOGRAPHY:	Dennis Greville

Except for the following supplied by Bill Ward: Vegetables and edible flowers, page 12; Picking garden, page 13; Marigolds, page 17; Feijoas, page 20; Daylillies, page 36; Nasturtiums, page 37; Lettuce, page 53.

ILLUSTRATIONS:	Rob Dileva

CONTENTS

5   Focused Planting

5   How to create an outdoor garden dedicated to edible plants

6   Gardening in smaller spaces

9   Edible plants in containers

11   Mixed Planting

11   Planting edible plants into an existing garden

14   The smaller mixed garden

15   Companion Planting

15   What is companion planting?

18   Companion planting guide

19   Fruits

19   Easy to grow varieties

21   Causes and remedies for common problems

31   Edible Flowers

31   Easy to grow edible flowers and how to use them

35   Flowering times of edible flowers

35   Causes and remedies for common problems

40   Vegetables – Leaf and Root Crops

42   Easy to grow varieties

45   Growing plants from seed – germination and planting times

47   Crop rotation for maximum results

50   Causes and remedies for common problems

54   Troubleshooting Charts

54   Insect pests

59   Fungal diseases

Introduction

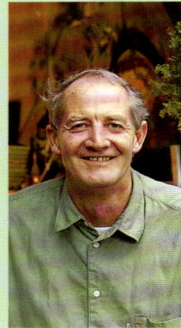

Everyone should grow at least a few edible plants – the taste of home-grown fruit and vegetables and the excitement of harvesting your own produce simply cannot be beaten.

From lemons to lettuces, cabbages to carnations, edible plants add variety not only in the garden but also when preparing and presenting food. It's a delight to be able to pick a bag of lemons to go with your gin or to give as a gift to help a friend combat a cold.

Space should not be a restriction when growing edible plants – some of the most innovative edible gardens I have seen have been container gardens. Most vegetables, flowers and fruits can be grown successfully in containers, hanging baskets, pots, barrels or even old baths. Given the right conditions, your plants will produce abundant crops to delight the palate.

Edible plants can be included as part of a herbaceous border or in a sunny spot among trees and shrubs. For those of us who do have some free space, creating a garden dedicated to edible plants will be most rewarding.

If you are new to growing edible plants, first choose plants you use regularly rather than growing the more unusual varieties. Pick easy to grow plant varieties – success definitely breeds success. In this book I share my thoughts on the more common varieties and tips on how to look after them, for excellent results.

In creating an edible garden, determine your own gardening style – if you have hours to spend every week then go all out. If you are more of a weekend or casual gardener like me don't grow plants that need a lot of attention (unless you put in place systems to ensure they get the attention they need – like a self-timing watering system).

Bon appétit,

Bill Ward

Focused Planting

How to create an outdoor garden dedicated to edible plants

Choosing the site and maximising the space

Ideally the site needs to be open, sunny and free-draining. Ensuring the soil is friable (loose, crumbly and easy to work) is one of the keys to successful gardening.

Any size garden from as small as half a metre square will enable you to grow your own crops. By creating a raised garden bed, you can even have a vegetable plot in areas that have no accessible digging space.

A simple raised bed ▼

This is relatively easy to do. Select your site then choose your edging material, eg. treated timber, sleepers or bricks. Ideally you need a height of 50-60cm. Once the edging is completed, part fill (to a depth of 5cm) with large gravel for drainage (ask at your garden centre). Then fill your bed with equal amounts of compost and soil or potting mix.

The soil

A loamy soil is ideal (fertile soil containing neither an excess of sand or of clay, and being rich in humus). If your soil type is predominately clay, dig in plenty of organic matter such as pea

A small patch can ▶ still meet most of your needs

straw, mushroom compost or peat. For sandy soil add some loamy soil, peat and compost in equal measures. Worms are an essential element for good growth as they help aerate the soil. A good source of worms is your own compost bin or, if you don't have one of those, try your local worm farm.

Watering, fertilising and feeding

Watering is essential for a successful garden. In a well-draining site you should water once a week in winter and every second day in summer (if very hot). Watch for any plants starting to wilt – this is nature's way of saying it's time to get out the hose.

Like people, plants need food if they are to grow. It amazes me how often I see home gardeners, who hope their vegetable patches will provide an abundant crop, have their expectations fall short simply because they failed to feed their plants regularly. Dig in compost, or use a balanced garden fertiliser. When planting your vegetable seedlings a light dressing of blood and bone is a must, followed every three weeks with a soluble liquid fertiliser.

HANDY HINT
If you are planning to use a terracotta pot or similar, paint the inside with teracoat (available at garden centres) before planting. This helps prevent the pot from drying out too rapidly.

Gardening in smaller spaces

- If space is limited still try to meet the essential requirements of an open, sunny and free-draining site with good soil.
- Almost all edible plants need lots of sun for success – ideally at least 6 hours on a good day.
- With a smaller site, plant your crops in rows or blocks to help facilitate pollination and maximise space – generally vegetables should be planted 20-30cm apart for best results. If you have a small garden then consider alternating your crops. For example, a row or block of beans then carrots, radishes then silver beet, lettuce then beetroot – a patchwork of colour that looks great.
- Rows should face east to west, to maximise heat from the sun.

■ Grow the taller crops where there is less likelihood of shade.

For a range of vegetables that provide the best yield for the least space, I suggest you consider the following: radish, dwarf varieties of beans and peas, beetroot, peppers, lettuce (especially the varieties where you can continually harvest a few leaves at a time like salad bowl or rocket), cherry tomatoes, cucumber, baby carrots, silver beet, spinach and many of the Oriental greens such as Bok Choy. All provide high nutritional value.

Don't waste space in summer with crops such as potatoes, cauliflower or cabbage. Potatoes at that time of the year are very inexpensive to buy and would take up too much room in a small plot. Cabbage and cauliflower are best planted in late summer and early autumn (to avoid the white butterfly menace), and provide quality greens during winter months. Don't forget leeks – they are an excellent crop to follow summer dwarf beans or peas.

All gardens, regardless of size, need to contain certain nutrients necessary for growth.

Use a good base dressing like Nitrophoska Blue or an all-purpose fertiliser at the rate of 25gms per square metre – most vegetables grow better in a sweeter soil.

To add style and colour to your vegetable plot, why not plant edible flowers like marigolds and violas amongst your vegetables, space permitting (see chapter on *Edible Flowers*). If you want to include fruit trees and vines in your plan, consider dwarf varieties (see page 19). Dwarf and semi-dwarf varieties can look fantastic when espaliered against a fence, or standardise your own apple or pear tree so you can plant underneath. Ballerina apples have been specifically bred for small gardens. Narrow and columnar in shape, the tree fruits on spurs, not branches. Hence they take up very little room. They also provide that important vertical element in your garden.

HANDY HINT
To fertilise root-bound pots, take a thick knitting needle, skewer or similar object and poke fairly deeply into the soil several times around the edge of the pot. Slow release fertiliser pellets such as Osmocote can then be dropped into these holes, helping to feed your plant.

An espalier tree (usually a fruit tree) has a vertical trunk from which lateral branches are trained horizontally. Espalier trees are often attached to walls, but can also be trained to wires strained between posts. A standardised tree needs a clear trunk so underplanting can be achieved – trim off lower branches over a period of time.

A specialised and self– ▲
contained garden

◄ *An espalier tree*

Edible plants in containers

Choosing containers

For successful growth I recommend planting in nothing smaller than a large bucket; the larger the container the better. Depth is also very important; plant shallow-rooted crops in at least 25cm. Potatoes and kumara will need something a little deeper – a wine barrel or similar sized plastic container is ideal for them. Anything less than 25cm deep dries out too quickly and watering becomes a problem. Grow bags are ideal when you have limited space or are surrounded by a concrete pad or balcony. 50 litre bags of potting mix work wonders when combined with a slow release fertiliser. In early summer I use these to grow tomato plants, a crop of lettuce and a few herbs.

Vegetables grown in containers will generally crop first ▼

Soil/potting mix

Shrub and Tub mix is essential for growing edible plants in containers as it is more free-draining than most other mixes. In addition it does not compact down and allows water and fertiliser to be easily absorbed and, as a bonus, is weed free. Using garden soil in containers can result in disease and weed growth (garden soil is not a sterile medium). The weeds may actually outgrow what you have planted!

Watering, fertilising and feeding

Containers need to be watered regularly – I recommend deep watering every second day during mild conditions and once a day during summer. (Always leave at least 2cm between the top of the soil and the top of your container – this stops water running off.) The best time to water is when the sun is off your pots – early morning and late afternoon. Adding a mulch of sphagnum moss, pebbles, bark, shredded newspaper or straw will help retain moisture in your containers.

When planting in containers I grow indicator plants such as violas, impatiens or alyssum nearby – when they wilt you know it's time to get out the hose again.

Vegetables that work well in containers include radish, dwarf beans, sugar snap peas, beetroot, peppers, lettuce (particularly any of the mesclun mixes), tomatoes, cucumber, baby carrots, silver beet, New Zealand perpetual spinach and Mizuna or Bok Choy from the Oriental varieties. Strawberries, blueberries and currants are also great. Most dwarf fruit trees, citrus (except oranges and grapefruit) and olives also work well. For specific details refer to later chapters.

DID YOU KNOW?
Vegetables in containers grow faster than those grown in the open ground. This is because the containers absorb and hold heat more readily – this stimulates and encourages plant growth.

Mixed Planting

Edible plants can be added almost anywhere in your garden – here are a few tips to ensure you get the best results.

Planting edible plants into an existing garden

Evaluate the site and choose plants that suit. The same rules of an open, sunny, free-draining situation apply. If your garden consists of trees and shrubs, and shade is not a problem, consider planting some small fruits in the gaps. Blueberries, currants, citrus, feijoas, olives and guavas will all work well. You can also grow dwarf apples, dwarf pears, tamarillos or avocados if space and climate permit. Be careful if you are considering planting in a shady spot. Most fruiting plants love the sun and will not thrive in shade. Spinach, celery and silver beet are some of the few plants that will semi-tolerate shade. Remember, most edible plants need a minimum of four and ideally six hours of bright sunlight per day.

In a herbaceous border (a border with lots of flowers) consider adding rainbow beet, beetroot, oak leaf lettuce, parsley, chives, calendula, roses, carnations, marigolds, standard citrus, olives and a few of the smaller growing fruit trees. These can be blended in easily and look great.

For a more formal effect don't dismiss the idea of taking a variety of fruit tree (say an apple) to standardise or espalier – for example, espalier a row of olive trees behind pink roses with a lamb's ear (stachys byzantina) border, creating a winning combination of silvers and pinks. Topiary is another great look.

The soil

Again anything other than clay or sand will work well. To increase soil fertility, add plenty of well rotted organic matter and dig in lots of compost. Sites where there are plenty of roots

HANDY HINT
To protect young seedlings from slugs and snails, place 1.5 litre plastic bottles with the bottoms cut off over each plant. Not only will this protect the plant, but the bottle acts as a mini glasshouse, encouraging growth.

Grow vegetables and edible flowers amongst trees and shrubs to maximise space ▶ ▶

Scarlet runner beans work well when grown in a barrel ▼

Even my mother's ▲
small picking
garden can be
used to grow a few
vegetables

from other plants should be avoided, as they will take the nutrients first and leave your new plants stunted.

Watering, fertilising and feeding

Deep watering is vital – that is watering the root ball with several litres, not just sprinkling the top 2 or 3 cm of soil. If you don't have much time, watering is best done by a controlled watering system. In early spring apply a dressing of a complete fertiliser at the rate of approximately 25gms per square metre (roughly a generous handful). Water well before applying and then again afterwards. This approach will avoid any fertiliser burn to other plants. Every two to three weeks apply a soluble liquid fertiliser to maximise growth and flavour.

The smaller mixed garden

As a guide, plant smaller edible plants in the front of your garden bed – either formally or informally, depending on the look you are trying to achieve. Lettuce, chives and radishes grown in clumps of three or five can provide good decorative colour (deep green to red for lettuce). For a formal look they can be used as an edging to a border (chives look great used this way). To ensure your garden maintains a formal look, crop harvesting needs a little thought and care to prevent patchiness. My suggestion is to take away every third plant to keep the continuity in the garden. If the beds are raised, consider planting a crop such as dwarf scarlet runners close to the edge - the beans look fantastic hanging over the side.

Once the front of your garden is planted, choose mid-sized plants to scatter throughout the rest of the patch – beetroot, silver beet, peppers, chillies, marigolds and larger growing flowers can also be used or mixed in. Containers of edible plants can look good when strategically placed in a small shrub garden.

Around your roses plant chives, lettuce, garlic, marigolds, nasturtiums, violas, beetroot, spring onions or radishes. To be daringly different, yams or parsley make a really good border.

HANDY HINT
Miniature roses look great in small vegetable patches. Flowering for nine months of the year, they are ideally suited for use in borders and they come in all colours including my favourite, Jade - a stunning blackish red.

Companion Planting

What is companion planting?

In short this is planting together crops that will derive some benefit from each other. There are some plants that will not thrive when grown near other plants, but there are also many that benefit each other. For example they may help to repel diseases, due to the aromatic scents they emit, or attract beneficial insects. Roots of some plants exude substances that can hinder or assist growth – for example, rosemary planted as a hedge or border will attract bees to aid in pollination, and repel slugs and snails. Mixed plantings are also less prone to pests and diseases than a mass planting of a single species.

Did You Know?

- Mint grown in pots and placed among cabbages will repel white butterfly.
- The onion family (chives, leeks and garlic) planted among leafy vegetables (lettuce, spinach and rhubarb) will dispel aphids.
- Rhubarb leaf spray is excellent for aphids and mildew. To make this spray you will need:

  1.5kg rhubarb leaves
  5 litres water
  15gm good quality soap flakes

  METHOD: *Boil the chopped rhubarb leaves for half an hour in 3.5 litres of the water, then strain. Dissolve the soap flakes in the remaining water and, when the rhubarb mixture is cold, add the two mixtures together.*
- Rhubarb leaves placed under cabbage, broccoli and cauliflower will inhibit clubroot.
- Radish, planted with carrots, will aid germination and reduce the task of thinning the carrot crop.
- Beetroot and kohl rabi grow well together – you can get two crops from one patch.

HANDY HINT
Garlic repels aphids and keeps away vampires (when was the last time you saw one?!) Planted around roses it works wonders, and the leaves are great added to salads and sandwiches.

HANDY HINT
Lavender planted near or around tomatoes or fruit trees aids pollination and fruit set. Flowering lavender attracts bees.

Garlic is a great ▲
companion to roses,
strawberries and lettuce

◄ Basil aids in tomato growth, and they taste great when combined in cooking

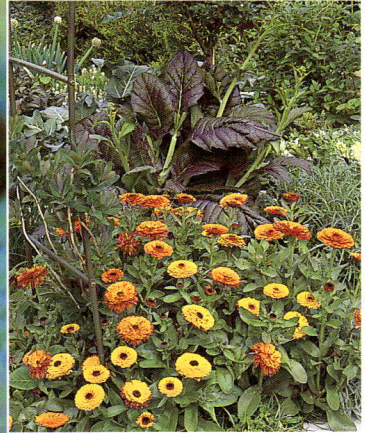
▲ Marigolds naturally disinfect the soil

▲ Compost – don't let the kitchen scraps go to waste

Companion planting guide

PLANT	BENEFICIAL COMPANION(S)	BAD COMPANION(S)
Apples	Chives, nasturtiums	Potatoes are hosts for blight
Asparagus	Tomatoes, parsley, basil	Potatoes compete for nutrients
Basil	Tomatoes, lettuce and most salad vegetables	Cabbage, cauliflower, pumpkins and large leaf vegetables
Beans	Potatoes, carrots, cauliflower, cabbage and celeriac	Onions, garlic and leeks all exude a substance that inhibits growth
Brassicas	Potatoes and celery do not compete for nutrients	Tomatoes and strawberries compete for food
Calendulas	Tomatoes and beans control whitefly, and protect tender crops from aphids	Pumpkins
Carrots	Peas, chives, tomatoes, lettuce, radish and marigolds	Dill
Celery	Leeks, tomatoes and brassicas	Silver beet are hosts for rust
Chives	Carrots, parsley and roses	Peas and beans
Corn	Potatoes, peas and beans	Tomatoes
Courgettes	Nasturtiums	Potatoes and aromatic herbs, eg. mint
Cucumber	Corn, peas and radish	Potatoes and aromatic herbs
French Marigold	Tomatoes and carrots—Butterball and Harmony are two hybrid varieties I recommend	None
Leeks	Onions, celery and carrots	Beans
Lettuce	Carrots, radish, strawberries and cucumber	None
Nasturtiums	Fruit trees	None
Onions	Strawberries and lettuce	Peas and beans
Parsley	Carrots and tomatoes	Peas and beans
Peas	Carrots, sweetcorn, beans and cucumbers	Onions, garlic and leeks
Potatoes	Beans, corn, cabbage and eggplant	Pumpkin (squash), cucumber, apples, raspberries and tomatoes
Pumpkin	Corn	Potatoes
Radish	Carrots, peas, lettuce and cucumber	None
Raspberries	Silver beet and beans	Potatoes (susceptible to blight)
Strawberries	Lettuce, onion and garlic	Eggplant and gladioli
Tomatoes	Chives, onion, parsley and asparagus	Potatoes, kohl rabi, broccoli and cabbage

Fruits

Fruit trees are not only for those with large gardens; there are many small to medium fruit trees, bushes and vines that adapt well to containers or smaller gardens. A large number of fruit trees are readily available as dwarf stock – this gives you the benefits of a larger tree on a smaller scale.

They include citrus, pears, apples, peaches, nectarines and cherries, some of which come with double and triple grafts - this gives you two or three varieties of fruit on the one tree. For example, a triple-graft apple tree could combine Cox's Orange, Gala and Granny Smith varieties, providing an early, mid and late season harvest. (Triple grafts are available only in apples, pears and peaches.)

Easy to grow varieties I recommend...

Citrus	Clementine mandarin	Round fruit, compact bush, good container plant
	Tahitian lime	Essential for gin drinkers
	Meyer lemon	Once established will fruit all year
	Kumquat	Purely ornamental, though fruit can be preserved in brandy – great dessert
Pip fruit	Ballerina apples	Bred especially for containers and small gardens – good colour and flavour
Stone fruit	Dwarf peach and nectarine	Grafted on 90 cm standards, produce succulent fruit
Guavas	Subtropical	Easy to grow and relatively disease free
Feijoa	Apollo	They topiary well and are great for coastal areas
Olive	Verdale	Never fails to please and can be espaliered or topairied

SMALL FRUITS AND VINES

Passionfruit	Crackerjack	Free cropping large fruit of good colour and pulp
Grapes	Black Hamburg	Excellent black fruit – ideal for growing over that north facing fence
Currants	Red, white or black	Red and black are more suited to warmer areas
Blueberry	Tasty Blue	My favourite
Fig	Brown Turkey	Adaptable, suits poor soils, can be grown in containers
Cherry	Stella	Upright, reddish fruits of good size
	Tang Shi (Dwarf)	Upright and hardy

Causes and remedies for common problems

The problems associated with fruit, and their remedies, have been categorised into 3 broad areas: poor growth; poor flowering and fruiting; and plants wilting, yellowing and dying.

For easy reference I have further divided this group of plants into the following categories: citrus, pip fruit, stone fruit, subtropicals, and small fruits and vines.

POOR GROWTH – CAUSES AND REMEDIES

Citrus

Frost hinders growth – ensure you use frost cloth or plant/transplant into a frost-free situation.

Stunted growth also occurs if the soil is heavy, poorly drained or lacks nutrients. To remedy, either raise the bed or dig in plenty of peat and sand to open up the soil. Citrus thrive in a free-draining soil rich in compost. Once planted avoid cultivation around the root area, as root disturbance will inhibit growth.

Lack of suitable plant food also results in poor or sluggish growth - for general health I feed my trees in March, September and December with 2kg per mature tree of a balanced fruit tree fertiliser such as Yates Citrus Fertiliser. I prune for shape when the crop has been harvested. Once this is done I spray with copper oxychloride to deter fungus. For other pests I generally use an oil spray in conjunction with Mavrik.

Pip fruit

To avoid stunted growth and diminished cropping in pip fruit such as apples, figs, pears and crabapples, you need to feed in August, December and April. Use Nitrophoska Blue at the rate of 100gms per square metre. Too often these applications are overlooked and cropping will begin to diminish, with the tree becoming prone to disease.

HANDY HINT
Don't prune citrus from October through February when borer beetle are on the wing. They attack damaged tissue, twigs, branches etc., and just love fresh cuts in trees.

◄ *Damson plums are one of my favourites* (MAIN PHOTO)

◄ *Feijoas – great for breakfast and in cakes*

Poor growth also occurs when trees are planted in poorly drained soils. All pip fruit must have free-draining soil - they will not do well in clay soils.

Small, spindly growth is often the result of not pruning or poor pruning. Pip fruit are best pruned in winter. Be careful to prune correctly to ensure you do not stunt the following season's growth.

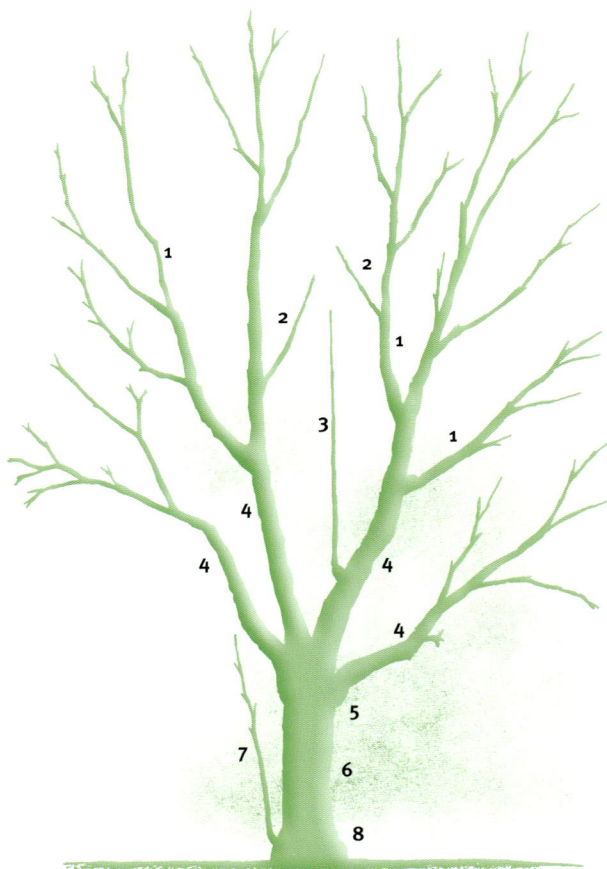

1 **Secondary Limbs**
2 **Laterals**
   The current season's growth, bearing fruit and leaf buds
3 **Watershoot**
   Fast growing laterals which are often unfruitful
4 **Main Limbs**
   The main branches or framework of the tree
5 **Crown**
   The point from which the main limbs are developed
6 **Trunk**
   Upright part of the tree between the ground and the crown
7 **Sucker**
   Laterals arising from below the bud union; normally cut off
8 **Bud or graft union**
   The point of union between the graft and root-stock
9 **Fruit buds**
   A bud producing flowers or flowers and leaves
10 Fruit spur
   A stubby growth bearing fruit and leaf buds

Pruning

Pruning needn't be difficult if you stick to the basics…

a) remove all dead and damaged tissue

b) remove any branches that cross over each other or are growing back into the centre of the tree

c) remove all watershoots (see no.3) and suckers (see no.7)

d) thin overcrowded growth and shape according to type

    Eg. **Plums** – cut long growth by two thirds

        Apples – cut to an outward facing bud. Reduce previous season's growth by two thirds.

        Peach and Nectarine – cut to outward facing double buds; triple buds are fruiting buds. (Both fruit on wood produced the previous season.)

Stone fruit

Stone fruit don't like heavy soils – again this stunts growth. They require generous applications of at least 1kg of a balanced fertiliser during spring, summer and autumn.

If your trees are not growing well, encourage strong growth by pruning peaches and nectarines in summer immediately after fruit set. Prune cherries, plums and apricots in mid winter. Be warned – pruning too hard will result in non-fruiting, whippy growth and the plant will take at least two seasons to recover.

If none of the above applies the problem could well be climatic. Most stone fruit need a cold winter to do well – if it's too warm your trees will produce short, spindly growth, resulting in poor fruiting.

Subtropicals

These grow easily and rapidly in frost-free regions but can wither and turn black if exposed to frost. A severe frost can even kill them. They are gross feeders and lack of food results in poor growth – apply a balanced fertiliser such as Nitrophoska Blue at the rate of 150gms per square metre in

September, December and again in March. (Rose fertiliser will also work and I often use it to feed both my roses and sub-tropicals at the same time.)

Prune to encourage new growth. Prune tamarillos in spring. Bananas are best pruned after they have finished fruiting – cut off at ground level to stimulate new growth. Other subtropicals can be pruned any time after fruiting.

Small fruits and vines

This covers plants such as brambleberries, blackberries, loganberries, grapes, kiwifruit and passionfruit, strawberries, blueberries, currants and gooseberries.

Feeding is important and the lack of it is the most common cause of poor growth. Apply fertiliser in September, December and March at the rate of a handful (150gms) per square metre. All dry fertilisers must be watered in well before and after application, as burning can occur if fertiliser is left in its raw state. Apply on an overcast day to prevent the sun burning the plants.

For vines apply the fertiliser along the whole length of the vine as this is where the feeding roots are travelling – this applies to all fruiting vines. A good fertiliser is Tui's Citrus Fertiliser which, as the name suggests, can also be applied to your citrus.

Badly pruned plants will also not grow to their potential. With the exception of passionfruit, prune all fruiting vines in winter. Passionfruit is best pruned in spring – they fruit on current season's growth. Grapes need to be pruned in mid winter otherwise they bleed – this inhibits the plant's ability to flower and fruit.

Gooseberries and currants don't do well in frost-free areas. They need a cold winter to firm the wood for the fruiting spurs. For success in warmer climates, throw a bag or two of ice around each plant's roots three to four times throughout the winter to aid in flower and fruit production.

HANDY HINT
Don't grow roses and apples together as they both host the fungal disease black spot - this can result in cross-infections which can be difficult to eradicate.

HANDY HINT
Sweet fruit can be achieved by regular feeding and a monthly application of a liquid plant food from spring to fruit harvest – it is well worth the effort.

Cherry Stella love cold climates ▶

POOR FLOWERING AND FRUITING – CAUSES AND REMEDIES

Citrus

Poor flowering and fruiting will result if the plant's roots have been disturbed – they will even drop their leaves, flowers, buds and fruit.

Soils too high in nitrogen will result in poor flowering – all foliage and no bud production. Dry, poor coloured fruit with no pulp (which may taste bitter) is symptomatic of a lack of potash.

Climatic variation (cold snaps during flowering) or a lack of pollination will result in a poor fruit crop. Wet feet over a period can also be to blame.

To produce sweet, juicy fruit prevent the soil around your trees from drying out too much in summer. Mulching with grass clippings works well so long as you don't place them too close to the trunk of the tree as this causes sweating and may start to rot the trunk.

Pip fruit

Cold nights at bud burst will affect pollination of flowers, resulting in bud drop. Pruning too hard will also result in a poor crop of fruit. Remember for most varieties fruit occurs on previous season's growth and spring growth does not produce fruit in that year.

To assist nature with pollination, plant rosemary, tansy or lavender. They will attract bees, who greatly assist pollination, and these plants also help to protect against codlin moth. As an alternative way of attracting bees, dissolve two teaspoons of sugar in 4 to 5 litres of water and spray over the tree while in flower.

Adverse climatic conditions and wet feet will cause stress on the plant, which may result in poor flowering.

Stone fruit

The biggest impediments to flowering are either pruning at the wrong time of the year or sudden climatic changes. Peaches and

DID YOU KNOW?
Magnesium and iron deficiencies occur in alkaline (or sweet) soils and where citrus trees have been planted too close to concreted areas. Avoid planting citrus near these areas or using concrete rings around the base of the trees as leaching of lime occurs, causing leaf discolouration.

nectarines are best pruned in summer after fruit set (when fruit has just formed) – this way you don't cut out your fruiting wood. Cherries, plums and apricots are best pruned in mid-winter – prune out all spindly, spent and dead wood and reduce the current season's leaders by two thirds. (See *Pruning,* page 23.)

In cold climates dwarf peaches and nectarines are good value for their flowering, fruiting and autumn display. They are not so good in humid, frost-free areas as they are vulnerable to pests and diseases – it is cheaper to buy the fruit than grow the tree!

Some stone fruit (including plums and cherries) need two or more trees in close proximity to crop as they are not self-pollinating. To strengthen the bud union and reduce the likelihood of flower drop during cold snaps, apply 100gms of sulphate of potash around each tree and water in well.

Adverse climatic conditions and wet feet also cause stress on the plant, which may result in poor flowering.

Subtropicals

Poor flowering and fruiting is due to it being too cold and/or the plants having wet feet. When watering subtropicals, drench, dry out and drench again. I always mulch with straw around the base, as this will conserve moisture in summer.

As gross feeders they need a lot of food to thrive – a straggly, undernourished plant will not perform. I find sheep manure applied regularly encourages vigour.

Very dry conditions will also stress the plant. This will put the plant into survival mode, diverting energy away from flowering and fruiting.

Small fruits and vines

To stimulate flower and fruit production, passionfruit, grapes and kiwifruit need an extra dose of fertiliser – 100gms of sulphate of potash mixed with 30gms of sulphate of ammonia applied in early spring. Try it, you'll be amazed by the results. Be careful though as too much fertiliser high in nitrogen will

HANDY HINT
A few copper nails hammered into the trunks of peach and nectarine trees reduces the incidence of curly leaf.

DID YOU KNOW?
Stone fruit need on average 150 litres of water every week in order to do well.

give lots of leaves and no flowers. Adverse climatic conditions, wet feet and poor pruning will also stress the plant, resulting in poor flowering.

Dry fruit is a result of lack of moisture during flower-to-fruit development. A fungal disease (dry berry) can then attack the tree, destroying the young fruit. Spraying with Bravo in early spring provides good control of this problem.

With strawberries, a longer than normal period (1-2 months) of fruit production can be attained by picking the first truss of flowers out of each plant. Doing this allows the plant to put its energy into root establishment, making a stronger plant, which will flower and fruit over a longer period.

PLANTS WILTING, YELLOWING AND DYING – CAUSES AND REMEDIES

Citrus

Continual root disturbance, or the plant's roots being wet for too long, will almost always result in wilting, yellowing and dying. If yellowing on leaves is a problem (some leaves may even drop) you can achieve deep green leaves again by applying half a cup of magnesium sulphate dissolved in a bucket of water distributed around the drip line. Early spring is the best time to do this. One dose should be enough for the average-sized tree.

If young citrus leaves are turning light green, yellow or even white, it is an iron deficiency. To remedy this, apply half a cup

Black Hamburg Grape – great along a sunny ◄ fenceline

of iron sulphate dissolved in 4.5 litres of water around the drip line (once a year should fix the problem). To prevent crystals forming, the iron sulphate is best dissolved in warm water.

Yellowing and wilting of leaves and stems leading to the collapse of citrus trees may be caused by borer – the borer lays its eggs into the soft tissue and the larvae hatches inside and starts feeding, causing weak stems that yellow, wilt and then snap off.

Container-grown citrus

Lack of food is the major reason for wilting and dying. Liquid feed with a water-soluble plant food. Mandarins, tangelos and some oranges are perfect to grow in large tubs, but grapefruit, due to its vigour, is a no no – they simply won't perform.

Drying out will stress the plant - this shows up as fruit and flower drop.

Pip fruit

If it is not wet feet, then the main reason for yellowing and wilt-ing of pip fruit is fungal or insect damage at the roots. Check by digging around the roots – if they are soft and mushy pull out the plant. (It is cheaper to buy a new tree than to try to combat disease with sprays.)

Never re-plant in the same spot unless you replace the soil. Dig out all surrounding soil to approximately 1 metre wide and 60cm deep and replace with fresh soil, then add Tricopel. This introduces bacteria to the soil, which protects the plant against fungus and stimulates plant growth. Yellowing and wilting can also be caused by borer, ultimately leading to the demise of your plant.

Stone fruit

Yellowing, wilting and collapse are usually due to wet feet or lack of nutrients. Stone fruit are more suited to cold climates – in humid climates they are often covered in a mass of yellowing leaves.

▲ *Lemons and limes are great in the garden, but also grow well in containers*

Subtropicals

Being too wet or too cold are the main reasons subtropicals wilt, yellow or die. If you can move the plant to a sunnier, sheltered spot, then do so. Subtropical fruit trees will collapse in most parts of the South Island, unless they are well protected

Yellowing and wilting could once again mean borer attack.

Small fruits and vines

If yellowing is not due to dryness or wet feet, this problem is generally the result of a fungus - either phytophera or fusarium wilt. This sometimes appears as a grey mould on strawberries. This problem can be readily addressed by spraying with Bravo.

Lack of nutrients will stunt growth and may result in yellowing and wilting – to avoid, feed regularly in early spring. Apply two heaped tablespoons of epsom salts to an average watering can or bucket and water along the length of the vine. Repeat in January.

Cold snaps or a sudden chill could also be to blame for your plants yellowing and wilting. Alternatively, high humidity over an extended period will likely result in the wilting of many small fruits. Fruiting will almost certainly be affected and, in severe cases, the plant may never recover.

HANDY HINT
Never use dry fertiliser, eg. citrus or fruit tree fertilisers, on trees grown in containers. The feeding roots are near the surface and will burn.

Common insects

Scale and aphids, thrips, codlin moth, mealy bug, pear slug and borer. Lacewing can be found on small fruits such as currants and gooseberries.

Common diseases

Curly leaf and brown rot are both commonly found, especially on peaches and nectarines. Verrucosis is found on citrus; black spot and mildew are especially common on tamarillos.

See *Troubleshooting Charts* (pages 54–62).

Edible Flowers

Introduction

The popularity of growing plants that produce edible flowers stems back to the earliest civilisations.

Today roses and orange flowers are commonly used as flavourings in the Middle East. In the Orient edible chrysanthemums, jasmine flowers and lily buds feature on daily menus. Squash flowers are also considered a delicacy. In French, Italian and now American cuisine, edible plants are also widely used.

The secret to using flowers as a food or in food is to experiment; add a little, then taste and see what you think – you can always add more.

Easy to grow edible flowers and how to use them

HANDY HINT
Many flowers can be added to ice cubes – they add colour and style to drinks and are great for childrens' parties. Red and pink rose petals frozen in ice and served with fresh orange juice never fail to draw comments. Make sure the flowers are well cleaned inside and out as an insect in your drink will never do!

Borage flowers

Great in cream, on scones, or used in desserts and jellies. Whole flowers look wonderful in leafy salads and are very flavoursome! The young leaves can also be used in salads – they have a cooling cucumber taste.

Calendulas

"Pacific Beauty" is my choice – it has the best orange colour of all and the strongest fragrance. Known as winter marigolds, they flower from late summer to spring. A few petals mixed into butter results in a sweet yet salty flavour – delightful! Use the petals in your scone mix, in salads, rice dishes or cold drinks. The orange of the petals provides a sharp contrast with many foods – used well it really dazzles.

Carnations

Clove varieties, such as "Mrs Simpkin", are a favourite – clove varieties are available in pink, red and white and are perennial.

The flower petals are tasty and really brighten a salad. They can be crystallised by dipping in a mix of egg white and castor sugar and then chilled – great as a topping for cakes and slices and wonderful with Pavlova!

Citrus flowers

All types. First used in Greek and Roman food, they are now a favourite with French chefs who drop them into cool drinks such as iced tea or summer wines. Use chopped or whole as a garnish with fish – superb. They also work well added to or on top of lemon or orange desserts such as cheesecake. Lemon flowers, added to old-fashioned recipes such as banana cake, add a fabulous zing.

Dandelions

Sometimes called "Poor Man's Chicory". Use young leaves and the flower petals to really liven up salads, while steeped flowers can also be used as a soothing tea. Pour boiling water over the flowers and drain – the tea is full of vitamins A, B, C and D and high in potassium. The roots can be used to make a beer and the leaves make a pleasant tasting wine.

Daylillies

From spring to late autumn they bloom like crazy. The buds and flowers are considered the most delectable part and can be deep-fried. (When using flowers remove anthers and stamens.) They have a pleasant nutty taste. Tightly closed buds can be used in salads, boiled, pickled or stir-fried. The young leaves stripped and broken up are great in salads or also in a stir-fry – they give a creamy onion flavour to the food. They are also delicious in egg dishes, go well with chicken and are a favourite additive in Chinese cooking.

French marigolds

Can be used in much the same way as calendulas, but are a little sharper in their taste.

DID YOU KNOW?
Josephine (Napoleon's lover) used to feast on carnations and loved roses in and accompanying her food. Cleopatra bathed in rose water, slept on a bed of lavender and dined on nasturtiums – why don't you?!

◄ *Violas and Oak Leaf Lettuce*

Lavender flowers

Stoechus hybrid forms like "Marshwood" are best, as they have larger petals or flags. They flower from spring to late summer. Flowers are used mainly to complement or enhance a sweet dish – use during cooking or as a garnish. Try mixing the flowers into cream or butter – a fabulous taste.

Nasturtiums

Gleam hybrids are ideal, as they are compact growers. Flowering from summer to winter, they have a peppery taste and are easy to grow as they thrive in poor soil. Nasturtiums can be added to salads, are great with asparagus (grill cheese on top of freshly cooked asparagus, then add a handful of nasturtium flowers to the top just before serving) and, in fact, are great accompanying any cheese dish or in a cheese sandwich.

Pumpkin, Squash and Kumi Kumi flowers

All the flowers from these plants are great. (Remove the anthers and stamens first.) The flowers (both male and female) are really great deep-fried (dip in egg and breadcrumbs). The buds are also used in Asian stir-fries.

Roses

Scented varieties are used in jams, jellies and baking. Add to a plain cake mix to give flavour or use as a topping on scones or cakes. Iced rose petal tea is great - add a handful of petals for each glass (pour over tepid water and then chill) and add sugar to taste if you wish.

Snapdragons

Snapdragon is the common name for antirrhinums. They are available in a range of colours, types and forms, from dwarf to those that grow a metre high. The flowers have a sharp flavour and suit salads. They are used as the sour in a sweet and sour dessert in many stylish American cafés and restaurants.

HANDY HINT
Rhubarb leaves placed in a 15cm deep trench will correct soils infected with clubroot.

DID YOU KNOW?
Marigolds look great and flower for months but they also aid in cleaning the soil - they exude a natural "disinfectant" that helps reduce and eliminate harmful plant organisms.

Violas

"Johnny Jump Up" is a great performer – it flowers from summer to autumn. Use in salads, desserts, jellies, as a topping to the jam on scones or to decorate drinks. Violas suit any sized garden and are great in containers.

Flowering Times of Edible Flowers

	JAN	FEB	MAR	APR	MAY	JUN	JUL	AUG	SEP	OCT	NOV	DEC
Borage	●	●	●	●					●	●	●	●
Calendula				●	●	●	●	●	●	●		
Carnation	●	●	●					●	●	●	●	●
Citrus			●	●	●	●	●	●	●	●		
Dandelion	●	●	●	●	●	●	●	●	●	●	●	●
Daylily	●	●	●	●	●					●	●	●
French marigold	●	●	●	●	●					●	●	●
Lavender*	●	●	●							●	●	●
Nasturtium	●	●	●	●	●				●	●	●	●
Pumpkin, squash & kumi kumi	●	●	●	●						●	●	●
Roses	●	●	●	●	●					●	●	●
Snapdragon	●	●	●	●	●					●	●	●
Viola/Pansy	●	●	●	●	●	●	●	●	●	●	●	●

*(stoechus varieties)

Causes and remedies for common problems

POOR GROWTH – CAUSES AND REMEDIES

All flowers require free-draining soil rich in humus and compost, or a well balanced container and tub mix. A friable soil is best, (this means it crumbles in your hand).

A sunny spot is essential as poor light results in straggly plants. Poor growth can also be a sign of soil exhaustion – particularly true if you are trying to grow the same plants in the same spot year after year.

Daylilies – all
parts are edible
and they have a
great peppery
taste ▶

Potted marigolds add colour to winter salads ▶

◀ *Nasturtiums – sensational in salads and so easy to grow*

Pumpkin flowers – great stir-fried or deep-fried ▶

Soils that are too dry or too wet can also be a problem, so check your situation carefully. Flowering plants do best in an open, sunny situation. Planting too early or in soil that is too cold can also result in poor growth.

Lack of water is a major factor inhibiting growth - flowering plants need warm weather and plenty of water to perform well. Drying out just once can stress the plant and it may take weeks for it to recover.

Planting in fresh compost or mushroom fertiliser will result in poor growth and may cause the plant to collapse. Compost needs to be left out in the fresh air for at least two weeks.

If none of the above applies and you still have stunted, straggly growth the problem is likely to be nutritional or from having a poor plant to begin with. Fertilise your plants regularly. I feed mine monthly, from spring through to late autumn, with a good base fertiliser such as Yates, Tui's or Debco's general garden fertiliser. If, after fertilising, you have no joy, discard the plant and replace with another species.

POOR FLOWERING AND FRUITING – CAUSES AND REMEDIES

Little or no flowering can be caused by extreme climate changes, eg. very cold nights followed by warm days. It could also mean you planted too early when the soil was not warm enough.

A lack of calcium, magnesium or potash will also result in poor flower production. These elements really need to be added to the base fertiliser when preparing the ground for planting.

Planting too close, or using too much blood and bone (rich in nitrogen) will result in all leaf and no flowers. Being too wet or too dry will stress the plant, causing it to collapse.

Flower drop can be caused by the plant's roots becoming too dry. Surface watering will – if followed by a hot, sunny day – scorch the roots, causing buds and flowers to fall or not

HANDY HINT
Potash helps flower-set, prevents bud drop and adds flavour to petals and leaves. Wood ash from open fires is an excellent means of supplying the necessary potash to soil - apply lightly throughout the year.

develop. A half-hour spray on a hot summer evening is never enough for an average-sized garden – deep watering every second day is needed.

PLANTS WILTING, YELLOWING AND DYING – CAUSES AND REMEDIES

Moisture on leaves on hot days will result in burnt leaves – not a good look. Plan to water your garden at the end of the day or use a trickle watering system.

Yellow leaves on a healthy plant generally point to nitrogen levels being low or possibly a magnesium and calcium deficiency. My quick fix is to apply sulphate of ammonia at 50gms a square metre, well watered in. If this is not effective try a light dosing of Dolomite at 25gms per square metre.

Climatic conditions can also cause problems – too wet or too dry will stunt and kill your plants. Like humans, plants do not react well to extremes; they need warm conditions and plenty of water.

Common insects

Scale, aphids, thrips, mealy bug, red spider mite, slugs, snails and caterpillars.

Common diseases

Mildew, rust and black spot.

See *Troubleshooting Charts* (pages 54–62).

See *Troubleshooting Charts* (pages 54–62).

HANDY HINT
Pick flowers early in the morning before the sun hits them - this is when they are at their prime for flavour. Picked in full sun, they become astringent. If you intend to use flowers later in the day, after picking put them in a shallow dish of water in a cool spot. Flowers generally do not freeze or dry well – fresh is always best.

Vegetables – Leaf & Root Crops

Nothing is more enjoyable than growing your own vegetables and nurturing them from seed to harvest. A wide range of ready-grown plants are also available from your local garden centre. If you are looking for something a little different however, King's seeds and other commercial seed merchants have a huge range of non-commercial varieties which are worth considering, such as heirloom vegetables and flowers. (Have you ever considered growing orange-striped tomatoes?!)

Sowing seeds in seed trays

Seeds can either be sown directly, (ie. straight into the soil) or in trays containing a quality seed raising mix. (Note that carrot, parsnips and radish do not transplant out well, so are best sown direct.) Fill your container to 1cm from the top and tamp down gently. Scatter seed lightly over the soil surface and, as a general rule, cover to the depth of the seed, (ie. the seed should only just be covered). Lightly water the surface with an atomiser sprayer, cover with glass and paper to maintain even moisture and heat, and place in a warm, sunny place in spring and in a warm, shady place in summer. Check regularly and remove the cover when the seed has germinated. Once the seeds have produced a pair of true leaves, they can be pricked out into other trays and, after three more weeks, they will be ready to transplant into the garden. (The first two leaves a seed produces are not true leaves. Prick out only after your seedling has grown its second pair of leaves.)

Sowing seeds in the garden

To ensure success, don't plant too deep – follow the instructions on the seed packet. Your sowing medium should be damp, not wet. Don't try and sow seeds too early (eg. pumpkin in late winter), as plants will fail if conditions are unsuitable. When

HANDY HINT
Where mineral deficiencies occur, an easy remedy is to apply trace element mix (available from your garden centre) once a year – preferably in spring. A 750gm pack will cover 45 square metres.

Maori Potatoes – easy ▶ to grow and well worthwhile

storing seed a cool, dry place is best, but if possible use fresh seeds as viability drops off after 6 months. Be alert for slugs and snails and control accordingly – don't apply any fertiliser until after transplanting, as you may burn the seedlings.

Today, even with reduced section sizes, you can still successfully grow your own vegetables.

Following is a chart covering some of the easy to grow varieties I recommend. In addition there are charts covering germination and planting times for these common varieties.

HANDY HINT
Crushed egg shell, placed around young seedlings, will protect them from slugs and snails.

Easy to grow varieties I recommend…

PLANT	VARIETY	COMMENTS
Beans	Golden Wax Scarlet Runner Top Crop	A sweet delight Perennial, excellent cropper Reliable performer
Beetroot	Cylindra Detroit Dark Red	Cylindrical Round with good form and colour
Bok Choy		Sow in autumn - excellent
Broccoli	Marathon	Once picked will crop again
Brussels sprouts	Emerald Ball	Firm heads
Cabbage	Golden Acre Red	Small and firm Holds well
Capsicum (Pepper)	Bell Boy	Green heavy cropper
Carrots	Topweight Manchester Table	Good colour Pale and sweet
Cauliflower	All Seasons	Good white – self-blanching
Celery	Dewcrisp Green	Crisp with excellent flavour
Chilli	Banana Red	Mild The hotter chilli
Chinese Cabbage	Chi-hi-Li	A great winter vegetable
Corn	Sugar Sweet Bantam Cross Honey & Pearl	My favourite Compact growers Widely used and very popular
Cress	Salad Curled	Quick and tasty
Cucumber	Telegraph Bush Crop Apple	Best grown on trellis Compact and produces well Freely produces

Eggplant	Early Long Purple	Crops well, large fruit
Endive	Green Curled	Good flavour and texture
Kohl rabi	Early Purple Vienna	Great in salads and stir-fries
Kumara	Ruawai Red or Yellow	Produces tubers of good size and texture
Leek	Musselburgh	Good texture and flavour
Lettuce	Iceberg	Firm heart, good texture and doesn't bolt to seed
	Mixed Oak Leaf	Available in a range of colours and perfect for a small garden – you should regularly pick a few leaves at a time and it will quickly regenerate
	Buttercrunch	Small, soft-hearted lettuce; ideal for sandwiches, mixed salads
Melon (Rock)	Hales Best	Succulent, fruits well
Parsley	Triple Curled	Compact grower, high in vitamins
	Italian	Sharper flavours
Parsnip	Supersnap	Good flavour and a reliable producer
	Hollow Crown	Holds well; slow to bolt
Peas	Onward	Good pods
	Sugar Snap	Best when young
Potato	Desiree (red)	Excellent for chips and other cooking
	Rua	Excellent main crop
	Maris Anchor	Keeps well; good cooking
Pumpkin	Buttercup	Earliest and free cropping
	Triamble/Crown	Stores well
Radish	Easter Egg	Colourful
	French Breakfast	Tapered red or white
	Red Globe	Round balls of red
Silver beet	Fordhook	A fabulous deep green colour
	Rainbow	Multi coloured – yellows, oranges and reddy-purples
Spinach	NZ	Pick the tips for year round nutrition
	Dutch Queen	Harvest whole plant
Spring onion	Spring Bunching	Good texture and firm, keeps well
Tomato	Sweet 100	Marble sized heavy crop
	Beefsteak	Large fruit, good flavour – great for sandwiches and grilling
Zucchini (courgette)	Black Beauty	Predominance of female flowers, therefore sets fruit more readily

HANDY HINT

Put a tablespoon of milk powder and a little potash under each tomato plant when planting - a great trick my Granddad passed on for really tasty tomatoes.

Germination times

VEGETABLE	Germination time (days)	Hints for success
Beans (Broad)	7–14	Soak for 2 hours before sowing
Beans (Climbing)	7–14	Soak for 2 hours before sowing
Beans (Dwarf & Runner)	6–10	Soak for 2 hours before sowing
Beetroot (Red and Yellow)	10–14	Soak for 24 hours before sowing
Bok Choy	6–8	Fresh seed is best
Broccoli, Brussels sprouts, Cabbage, Cauliflower	10–14	Fresh seed is best
Capsicum (Pepper)	6–14	Pre-chill*
Carrot	14–21	Sow direct to your garden rather than using a seed tray – they do not transplant well
Celery	10–21	Pre-chill*
Chilli	5–7	Ideal soil temperature around 15°
Chinese Cabbage	6–8	Sow direct
Corn	8–10	Soak overnight
Cress	7–10	Keep moist
Cucumber	5–10	Pre-chill*
Eggplant	7–14	Pre-chill*
Endive	7–14	Keep moist, pre-chill*
Kohl rabi	12–15	Keep moist, pre-chill*
Leek	6–14	Pre-chill*
Lettuce	7–10	Pre-chill*
Melon (Rock)	4–8	Soak for 6 hours before sowing
Melon (Water)	4–14	Soak for 6 hours before sowing
Onion	10–14	Sow direct
Parsley	10–28	Soak for 2 hours before sowing
Parsnip	10–28	Pre-chill*, sow direct to garden
Peas	7–10	Soak for 4 hours before sowing
Pumpkin	5–10	Soak for 4–6 hours before sowing
Radish	4–6	Sow direct to garden
Silver beet	6–14	Wash seeds & soak 1-2 hours
Spinach	7–21	Pre-chill*
Spring onion	6–10	Sow direct
Tomato	3–14	Ideal soil temperature 15°
Zucchini (courgette)	7–14	Soak for 4–6 hours before sowing

* To lightly pre-chill seeds, place in the fridge for 2 days.

Planting times (Seeds or Plants)

Crop	Jan	Feb	Mar	Apr	May	Jun	Jul	Aug	Sep	Oct	Nov	Dec	Approx. picking week
Beans (Broad)				•	•	•	•						14
Beans (Climbing)	•									•	•	•	16
Beans (Dwarf)	•									•	•	•	10
Beetroot	•	•	•						•	•	•	•	16
Bok Choy				•	•	•	•	•	•	•			8
Broccoli	•	•	•	•	•			•	•	•	•	•	16
Brussels sprouts	•	•	•	•								•	24
Cabbage	•	•	•	•					•	•	•	•	16
Capsicum (pepper)									•	•	•	•	16
Carrot	•	•	•	•				•	•	•	•	•	18
Cauliflower	•	•	•	•	•	•	•	•	•	•	•	•	18
Celery	•								•	•	•	•	18
Chilli	•	•	•							•	•	•	16
Chinese Cabbage				•	•	•	•	•					9
Corn										•	•	•	14
Cress	•	•	•	•	•	•	•	•	•	•	•	•	9
Cucumber									•	•	•	•	12
Eggplant										•	•		18
Endive				•	•	•	•	•	•				6
Kohl rabi	•	•	•	•									18
Kumara										•	•	•	22
Leeks	•	•	•							•	•	•	26
Lettuce	•	•	•	•	•	•	•	•	•	•	•	•	9
Melons										•	•	•	12
Onions				•	•	•	•	•	•				26
Parsley	•	•	•	•	•	•	•	•	•	•	•	•	9
Parsnip	•	•								•	•	•	26
Peas	•	•	•				•	•	•				14
Potato	•						•	•	•	•	•	•	15
Pumpkin									•	•	•	•	22
Radish	•	•	•	•	•	•	•	•	•	•	•	•	6
Silver beet	•	•	•	•	•	•	•	•	•	•	•	•	12
Spinach				•	•		•	•	•				12
Spring onion	•	•	•	•	•	•	•	•	•	•	•	•	10
Tomato	•									•	•	•	12
Zucchini (courgette)										•	•	•	12

Crop rotation for maximum results

If you grow the same crops in the same spot every year, two problems occur. Firstly, soil-living pests and diseases will increase. As an example, planting brassicas (cabbage family) every year in the same area will cause the root fungal disease known as clubroot to occur. This manifests itself as stunted growth, twisted foliage and, when dug out, the roots will be gnarled. To remedy this, add 250gms of lime per square metre during winter. There is also a commercial spray, Green Guard, which is used as a drench to help alleviate the problem.

Secondly, nutrient levels will become unbalanced and growth will become stunted or malformed. Examples include tomato plants with distorted top leaves (this generally indicates a lack of calcium in the soil) and cauliflower starting to pink on the leaves or head, suggesting a lack of phosphorus. An application of superphosphate at 100gms per square metre will address the nutrient imbalance.

But the best way to prevent these problems is to rotate your planting. An easy guide is outlined in the following chart. Simply identify your last crop and follow the chart. For example, a brassica crop in the first year is followed by a root crop the next.

Year 1	Year 2	Year 3	
Roots	Others	Brassicas	
Brassicas	Roots	Others	
Others	Brassicas	Roots	
Root Crops	**Brassicas**	**Others**	
Beetroot	Bok Choy	Beans	Melon
Carrots	Broccoli	Capsicum	Parsley
Kohl rabi	Brussels sprouts	Celery	Peas
Kumara	Cabbage	Chilli	Pumpkin
Leek	Cauliflower	Corn	Silver beet
Parsnip	Chinese Cabbage	Cress	Spinach
Potato		Cucumber	Spring onion
Radish		Eggplant	Tomato
		Endive	Zucchini
		Lettuce	

Beetroot leaves and roots are edible raw or cooked ▲

◄ Oriental vegetables grow well in small spaces

Silver beet is one of the few vegetables that tolerate shade ▼

Causes and remedies for common problems

POOR GROWTH – CAUSES AND REMEDIES

Poor soil is the major culprit. All vegetables enjoy a rich, organic soil or potting mix. A friable soil is best, as is a sunny spot.

Poor, straggly growth can be caused by buying seedlings that are too old (small is best). Larger plants are usually root-bound and stressed and, when planted in your vegetable patch, will just sit there before bolting, going straight to seed. Lack of growth can also be a sign of soil exhaustion – this occurs when the same crop has been planted in the same spot year after year, (see *Crop Rotation*, page 47).

Too dry/too wet or not enough sun can also be to blame, so check your situation carefully. Vegetables do best in an open situation – they hate shade. Planting too early, or in soil that is too cold or too hot, can also be a problem. For example, capsicum, tomatoes, pumpkins and watermelons need a ground temperature of 15°C to survive and grow well.

Stunted, straggly growth can also be caused by a lack of nutrients. Fertilise regularly – I feed my vegetable plants monthly with a good base fertiliser.

Green crops such as lettuce, cabbage, cauliflower and brussels sprouts need plenty of nitrogen for good growth. A light handful of blood and bone when planting, followed by a good handful or two of sheep pellets 3-4 weeks later, is ideal. Liquid fertiliser is also a good option.

If your plants are flowering but lack bulk then your ground is probably too rich in nitrogen. You need to balance the soil by putting on 15gms per square metre of superphosphate, or a good dosing of general garden fertiliser, say 25gms per square metre.

Stunted, straggly growth can also be caused by using too much fertiliser or organic matter: the soil becomes too rich. It's

HANDY HINT
For really sweet, crisp lettuce add a teaspoon of epsom salts to each plant two to three weeks after planting, and again two to three weeks later.

like eating too much chocolate cake – it's just too rich and overeating will soon start to make you feel sick. Stunted growth can also appear as misshapen roots in carrots, parsnips, kumara and potatoes, and is usually caused by clay or heavy soil.

Root crops such as beetroot, radish, parsnips, carrots, potatoes and kumara require more phosphate and less nitrogen. (You could end up with all top and no root this is known as 'bolting'.) Apply superphosphate at a rate of 50gms per metre before planting, but work it in well.

Fruiting crops that colour such as tomatoes, capsicums and pumpkins enjoy more potash than most – it is essential for fruit set and colour.

A well-balanced soil is important for other fruiting crops such as cucumbers and beans. Deep watering is also vital, as is a good dose of Nitrophoska Blue every second month. Don't forget regular liquid feeding.

Thick skins on vegetables usually means your calcium levels are too low – apply Dolomite to rectify.

Irregular watering, especially over summer, can also cause problems with growth. Too much water, followed by too little, leads to stress and stunted growth.

Overcrowding and over cultivation (eg. disturbing the roots of the plant when hoeing the ground) will also result in stunted growth.

POOR FLOWERING AND FRUITING – CAUSES AND REMEDIES

As mentioned previously, little or no flowering can be caused by extreme climate changes, eg. very cold nights followed by warm days. It could also mean you planted your crop too early, when the soil was not warm enough.

A lack of pollination will cause poor fruiting, or it could be too much nitrogen in the soil, meaning all leaf and no flower. Tomatoes, pumpkins and courgettes can all be pollinated by hand. To do this get a child's paintbrush and brush inside the open flowers, moving brush from flower to flower. Also

HANDY HINT
I use the tops of my beetroot as a vegetable – two crops for the work of one. Tear foliage rather than cutting it (cutting causes the crown to bleed, reducing the nutritional value) for a tasty delight that is great in salads.

HANDY HINT
I plant basil around my tomatoes. Basil thrives on the same fertiliser and soil conditions. It dispels aphids, fruit fly and, to a degree, whitefly. Basil flowers attract the bees that will aid the fruit set of tomatoes.

remember your base fertiliser should include calcium, magnesium or potash to help flowering and fruit production.

Flower drop is caused by the plant's roots becoming too dry. Surface watering will, if followed by a hot, sunny day, scorch the plant's roots. I recommend either a soaker hose or watering system. Flower drop from lack of water often happens to beans and peas.

PLANTS WILTING, YELLOWING AND DYING – CAUSES AND REMEDIES

Avoid watering during the heat of the day to minimise burning of leaves.

Bronzing or pinking on the outer edges of foliage is often seen on cauliflower, cabbages, broccoli, brussels sprouts and swedes. This is an indication of a nutritional imbalance. Remedy by applying 50gms of superphosphate per square metre.

Yellow leaves on a healthy plant generally point to nitrogen levels being low, or possibly a magnesium and calcium deficiency.

Common insects

Lacewings, caterpillars, aphids, slugs, thrips, green vegetable grub, whitefly, millipedes.

Common diseases

Blight on tomatoes and potatoes, rust on silver beet, leaf spot on celery, mildew on all cucubit (pumpkins, cucumbers and the like).

See *Troubleshooting Charts* (pages 54–62).

*Lettuce is easy to ▸
grow in containers*

Troubleshooting – Insect Pests

Problem	Symptom	Treatment	Natural Treatment
Aphids & Woolly Aphids	Small oval-shaped insects usually in clusters on tip growth. Cause distortion, stunted growth and loss of vigour to plants. Attack fruit, vegetables, ornamentals – even weeds.	- Mavrik (a bee friendly chemical spray).	- Pyrethrum or garlic spray - Wash over with soapy washing water (cold of course). - Squash by hand. - Ladybirds – they eat 400 a week.
Borer	Borer larva tunnels and destroys stem tissue, causing stems and limbs to weaken and die. Attacks citrus, fruit trees, small fruits and a raft of ornamentals. Distinguished by sawdust-like deposits on stems and bark.	- Conqueror Oil (all seasons) spray. - Inject with Kiwicare borer injector fluid.	- Conqueror Oil. - Kerosene poured into entrance holes. Seal with petroleum jelly.
Butterfly (White)	Attacks cabbage, cauliflower, broccoli, swedes, brussels sprouts. Reduces leaves to skeletons. Caterpillars are dull green in colour and voracious eaters.	- Carbaryl. - Pyrethrum. - Derris Dust.	- Squash by hand. - Make up spray by boiling lettuce leaves – cool and apply at rate of 1 to 3.
Carrot Rust Fly	Young seedlings of carrots, parsnips, celery and parsley are stripped bare and it attacks from seedling to maturity.	- Diazinon.	- Jeyes Fluid. - Wind break. - Soapy washing water.
Codlin Moth	Adults fly from October through November. They lay eggs from which caterpillars emerge and attack pip fruit (pears, apples, quince) and related ornamentals.	- Critical to spray October, December and January. - Malathion Spray. - Diazinon granules.	- Corrugated cardboard impregnated with Petroleum Jelly then attached to trunk of fruit trees. - Plant tansy, woodruff at base.

Troubleshooting - Insect Pests

Problem	Symptom	Treatment	Natural Treatment
Grass Grub	This root-eating larva of beetles is evident from February to May, causing extensive turf damage.	- Diazinon granules.	- Corrugated cardboard impregnated with Petroleum Jelly then attached to trunk of fruit trees.
Green Vegetable Grub	A severe pest of vegetable and garden plants. Loves beans. Distinctive bright green in colour.	- Mavrik insecticide. - Malathion insecticide. - Carbaryl insecticide.	- Squash by hand. - Pyrethrum and garlic spray.
Leaf Hopper	White flecking on foliage – often present on the underside of leaves. Hop amongst foliage when disturbed.	- Pyrethrum.	- Garlic spray - Cold, soapy washing water applied daily until infestation controlled.
Leaf Roller Caterpillar	A surface chewing caterpillar found on fruit trees and ornamental plants. Causes major damage to late fruiting crops resulting in secondary fruit rot.	- Carbaryl.	- Squash by hand. - Pyrethrum and garlic spray.
Mealy Bug	White fluffy insect which causes debilitation and stunted growth. Affects house plants, ornamentals, fruit trees, cacti, palms.	- Confidor (spray or drench). - Maldison and oil.	- Methylated Spirits on paint brush.
Passion Vine Hopper/Lacewing	Yellow to pale green in colour with bell shaped wings - causes severe foliage damage.	- Mavrik (bee friendly insecticide).	- Pyrethrum and garlic spray.
Pear Slug	Small, black, slimy slug which strips the green off leaves - attacks a wide range of ornamentals and cherry, plum and pear trees.	- Malathion. - Carbaryl.	- Pyrethrum and garlic spray.

Peach leaf ▶
curl – apply
copper

Rhubarb – ▶
don't waste
the leaves,
use them as a
spray (see
page 15)

◄ Mildew –
baking soda
will fix it

◄ Leaf Hopper
- dose with
garlic and
chilli spray

Troubleshooting – Insect Pests

Problem	Symptom	Treatment	Natural Treatment
Scale Insects (Sooty Mould)	Excretion of scale insects - looks like blackish soot.	- Combination of all seasons oil and Malathion gives good chemical control.	- Wipe off foliage with rag dipped in milk or all seasons oil wash.
Slugs and Snails	Member of octopus and oyster family - love the damp. They cause severe damage to newly planted flower plants, vegetables and seedlings along with a broad number of ornamentals and succulents.	- Mesurol/Baysol.	- Egg shells, crushed and placed around young seedlings. - Flat beer in saucers. - Pick them up at night with a torch and put them in a bucket of hot water, or crush them.
Spider Mite	Spider mites are rec in winter. They cause severe stunting and discolouration. Affect herbaceous and woody plants and vegetables.	- Mite Killer.	- Keep plant foliage atomized with water.
Thrips	Pin-size black insects found feeding on the sap on the underside of leaves, resulting in characteristic silvering of foliage. Attack a wide range of plants.	- Confidor is best, or Spraying oil and Malathion.	- Remove affected material.
White Fly	Miniature white sap-sucking moth-like insects which attack almost any plant growth including vegetables, fruits, ornamentals and weeds.	- Confidor - Target.	- Kodak yellow paper hung with a coating of Petroleum Jelly.

Troubleshooting – Fungal Diseases

Problem	Symptom	Treatment	Natural Treatment
Blight	Brown fungal patches on leaves and stems.	Spray with Copper Oxychloride or Bravo.	Pick off affected leaves and burn. Copper wire through stems.
Botrytis (grey mould)	Occurs in damp, warm and humid conditions. Attacks leaves, stems and fruit, causing rot. Due to overcrowding and poor ventilation. Seen as greyish mould.	Thiram / Saprol. Spray every 14 days where infection is evident.	Dust with flowers of sulphur. Open up infected area. Where practical remove affected material.
Brown rot on peaches, nectarines, apricots and plums	All stone fruit can be affected in spring. Flowers/immature fruit often take on a mummified appearance.	Spray with Saprol.	Collect and burn affected material.
Citrus brown rot	Leaves wilt and turn brown and fruit has brown rotting patches. Prevalent during late autumn and winter.	Copper Oxychloride. Spray early autumn, then monthly until spring.	Garlic, chilli and onion spray.
Die-back (shot hole)	Attacks leaves, fruits and twigs. Can cause scabs on fruit.	Copper spray in winter.	Cut out infected material and burn.
Downy mildew	Wet weather disease on grapes and vegetables. Appears as small, angular cream to brown spots.	Manzeb. Spray at first sign of infection and again 10 days later.	Pick and burn affected foliage.
Leaf curl Bladder plum	Leaves curl as they unfold – severe on stone fruits – causing defoliation and fruit drop. In plums seen as deformed and bladder-like fruit.	Copper spray. Winter, autumn and spring.	Cut out infected leaves and fruit.

Sooty Mould – fix
with oil ▶

Liquid fertilisers –
always useful ▼

Snail – flat beer in a saucer works well ▼

Caterpillar damage – derris dust to the rescue ▼

Troubleshooting – Fungal Diseases

Problem	Symptom	Treatment	Natural Treatment
Leaf spot/Black spot	Causes distorted growth and spotting on apples and pears. In severe cases leaf/fruit drop occurs.	Spray with fungus fighter.	Collect and burn affected material as dormant spores over winter will reinfect spring growth. A dusting of flowers of sulphur will help.
Powdery mildew	Appears as a white powdery covering on young leaves, fruits, and vegetables, eg. tamarillos. Occurs in dry seasons and dry climates.	Bravo. Spray every 14–21 days during summer.	Two teaspoons of baking soda per 2.5 litres of water.
Pythium. Damping off – on seedlings	Sudden collapse of young seedlings.	Spray with Captan.	Poor light, ventilation and drainage are generally the cause. Rectify the situation and hey presto, success.
Rust	Brown or reddish pustules on underside of leaves.	Spray with Zineb.	Pick off affected leaves. Dust with flowers of sulphur.
Verrucosis	Distorted lesions on the skin of citrus.	Spray with Copper Oxychloride after fruit set.	Pick off affected fruit.

Basic Spray Guide

Here is a basic spray guide for these commonly grown pl...
Insect pests, fungal diseases and their treatments are covered in
greater detail in the *Troubleshooting Charts* on pages 54–62.

Plant	When to spray	To protect against	Type of spray
Tomatoes	Sept – Oct	Blight, Bacterial Speck	Copper Oxychloride
	Nov – April	Early, late Blight, Leaf Mould, Botrytis, White Fly, Tomato Fruit Worm, Caterpillars & Aphids	Bravo & Orthene
Currants & Gooseberries	Late July	Scales & Mites	Conqueror Oil
	Bud movement	Leaf Spot	Copper Oxychloride
	Pre-blossom	Fungal diseases, Caterpillars	Copper Oxychloride, Orthene
Grapes	August	Scales, Mites, Mildew, Black Spot	Oil
	Bud swell	Scales, Mites, Mildew, Black Spot	Copper Oxychloride, Orthene
	Bud burst, pre-blossom, post fruit set & at 14 day intervals	Downy Mildew, Powdery Mildew, Black Spot	Bravo
	Post fruit set	Leaf roller, Aphids, Mealy Bug	Target
Stone fruit	Dormant	All fungal diseases	Copper Oxychloride
	Bud swell	Leaf Curl, Bladder Plum	Copper Oxychloride
	Bud burst	Leaf Curl, Bladder Plum	Copper Oxychloride
	Full bloom	Brown Rot	Saprol
	Petal fall	Brown Rot	Saprol
	3 weeks later	Brown Rot	Saprol
	3 week intervals to harvest	Brown Rot, Oriental Fruit, Moth & Cherry Pear Slug	Saprol, Carbaryl
	During leaf fall	All fungal diseases	Copper Oxychloride
Citrus	October	Verrucosis, Melanose, Aphids	Copper Oxychloride, Orthene
	November (petal fall)	Verrucosis, Aphids	Copper Oxychloride, Orthene
	December (after flowering)	Verrucosis, Aphids, Scale, Red Mite, Mealy Bug	Copper Oxychloride, Orthene and Conqueror Oil
	February	Verrucosis, Aphids, Scale, Red Mite, Mealy Bug	Copper Oxychloride, Orthene and Conqueror Oil
	April	Verrucosis, Aphids, Mealy Bug	Copper Oxychloride, Orthene
	May	Verrucosis, Aphids, Mealy Bug	Copper Oxychloride, Orthene
	June	Verrucosis	Copper Oxychloride

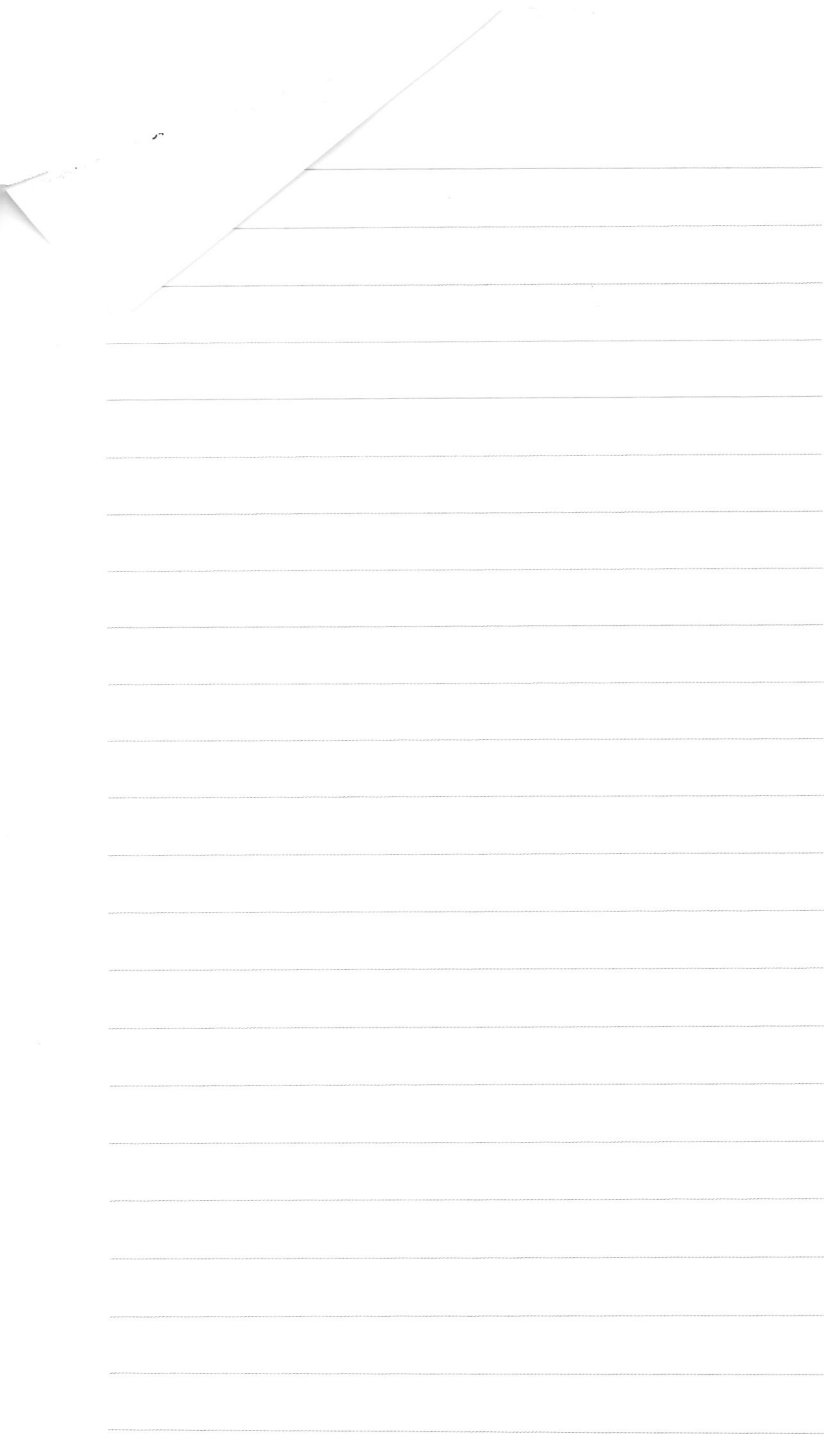